TEMPEST
PULS

DEDICATION

To Liz

Thank you,

my friend,

For the decades

of laughter,

lunches and

loyalty.

TABLE OF CONTENTS

TABLE OF CONTENTS continued

TABLE OF CONTENTS continued

TABLE OF CONTENTS continued

COPYRIGHT AND DISCLAIMERS

FOREWORD

One of the greatest compliments
That people pay me is to say
"I can write poems like yours".

It is a compliment,
Because it means my words
Are read and understood.

It is a compliment,
Because it means my words
Have been considered.

It is a compliment,
Because it means my words
Have an audience.

My advice to anyone
Wanting to write
Is to find your own voice.

Write in the style
That you find comfortable
And be honest and open.

Being authentic
Is where truth is revealed,
A gift to be given freely.

ABOUT THE AUTHOR

There are times
when I wonder
if growing older
creates less passion,
a dialling down of
the tempestuous pulse.

I think not
I hope not
yet, not all emotion
is joyful, but without
anguish, would I know
happiness in later life?

WORDS

I am full of words
Sometimes

When I write
them down in poems

I hope someone
will read one or two

And then feel
less alone

WORDS IN THE DICTIONARY

Flicking through the dictionary,
because the spell-check kept
changing what she had written
to something with a different sense.

She spotted words
that caught her eye,
Appealed in their sound,
sparked her imagination:

Bruxism, which is the habitual
Grinding of the teeth

Chiffchaff being a small warbler
Codswallop meaning nonsense

Globigerina a minute
marine creature

Pedicab describes a light vehicle
of three wheels

Shakudo, which is an alloy
of copper and gold

And zilch, meaning
zero or nothing at all.

THANK YOU LETTER

I just wanted to say thank you
for the basket of fruit;
It was such a lovely surprise.

The nectarines are plump,
the cherries deeply glossy,
and the apples crisp and green.

It's the first time that
I've received such a gift,
making it extra special.

I very much appreciate
the time and trouble
you must have taken.

I am delighted
that my suggestions
helped you get the job.

LISTEN

There is no one to listen
even when
I start to speak.
Everyone wants
to air their views,
Give themselves a voice.

There is no one to listen,
although I need to talk,
I just want to be heard.
Why can't people
just shut up
and listen?

TEMPESTUOUS PULSE

In the air is a tempestuous pulse
It beats with exaltation
It throbs with intensity
Its rhythm is raging.

All around is the disturbance
Of wildness
Of feverishness
Of tumult.

It is a state of violent commotion
A passion
An uproar
A storm.

It is the fury that drives change
The confusion of emotions
The drive for action
The volcano erupting.

AGITATED

The tempestuous pulse is
the agitation of
intense emotion.

The tempestuous pulse affects
mood either to be
creative or aggressive.

Perception of time
is distorted, making
it seem faster or slower.

A tempestuous pulse
leads to reckless action
or earthly paradise.

BLOOD LUST

The air was stagnant
with strips of static cloud,
hanging in the sky.
The fog of war
was weaving its spell.

The villagers had fled
to the ancient catacombs
in a desperate attempt
to avoid the marauding
and murderous soldiers.

The battle was over,
yet these men were not sated
by the death they had wrought,
nor satisfied with the
destruction they meted out.

The soldiers lusted
for more blood, any blood.
So the people hid
until madness passed
and sanity returned.

BATTLE BLOOD

I was walking along the road.
The wind was blowing cold,
but it wasn't icy enough
to cool the raging tempest
erupting within me.

In that moment, I was
the warrior queen, Boudica,
feeling the battle blood
surging through my veins,
a match for any Roman.

My feet stomped
heavily on the ground.
In a Hollywood movie
I would have left
deep, dark holes.

I was not in the mood
for people, not anyone.
It was lucky then
the road was empty,
even the pigeons kept away.

It is hard to maintain
so much passion for long.
It seeped away slowly
with each crashing footfall.
My gift to the earth.

WINGS AND HORNS

I have wings

I have horns

I am the duality
that is a mortal being

I am the whole of it.

PONDERING ON
WINGS AND HORNS

I have wings
I can soar with angels

I have horns
I can fight demons

I have a heart of gold
I have feet of clay

I am little, old me.

DEMOCRACY

In the news are stories
that democracy is under threat.
The silent majority
no longer relate to their MPs

Out of touch

These modern representatives
have lost their moral judgement,
hiding behind small print
in a wishy-washy code of conduct

Greedy

They are no longer role models,
seeking to manage with honour.
Instead, they are egotistical
and self-serving, without shame

Vain

They regularly increase their salaries
and yet suppress pay for others.
Their behaviour is their message:
We will not be judged by voters

Arrogant

There are also good MPs,
yet whilst they do nothing
they are part of the problem
they need to do much more

Silent

LOVE

When you are in love,

heart rate increases,

blood pressure rises,

glands release adrenaline.

How is that romantic?

SUCH IS LOVE

In so short a time
How can I know you?
Yet I do.
At other times
I just want to spend
the rest of my days
exploring you.

AND YOU

When I think of you
Are you thinking of me?

When I dream of you
Are you dreaming of me?

When I am loving you
Are you loving me?

SEARCHING

In the early morning mist
I look for your face,
hoping to see that slow, lazy smile.

In the golden rays of the sun
I remember your warmth
and the touch of your hand.

In the silver beams of the moon
I search for the magic
of our shared existence.

In the soft cooling of the breeze
I strain to hear your voice,
sharing some silly joke.

In the gentle falling of the rain
I hide my pent up tears
so you will not know my sorrow.

MY WARM LIGHT

I know you are there
among the stars.
A warm light
in the night sky.

You will not be too far
from me or I from you.
We both wait for
a different life to begin.

HOME

Any distance is never too far to travel

when the destination is my happy place.

It is home and that home

is wherever you are in the world.

HAUNTED

I wonder if I try to capture you
whether you will disappear
like fragile mist in summer.

You haunt me now you are dead
as you never did before, because
in this life, you let me go.

You set me free with
a smile and good wishes,
a happy ending to our love.

When I did remember
to think about you
it was a fragile memory.

Yet, you haunt me now,
perhaps you are trying to
tell me something.

I cannot hear you,
I can only see you
and wonder.

BLACK DOG

The black dog keeps me company
He is insistent in his attention
He is arduous in his pursuit.

The black dog is not warm
He does not have a care of me
His presence is not reassuring.

BACK FOR MORE

Here you are again,
back for more,
even though
last time you said
it would would never
happen again.
You took all that I had,
leaving me empty.
But now
you are back for more.

STRUGGLING

Hello, I'm struggling here:
My shoulders are stiff and sore
My heart is a leaden weight.
I would mention it to you,
but your weary sighs stop me.
I hear you slamming about
in your own private fury.

I can't stand this any more:
The weather is bleak
I am very tired
and I only see gloom.
I have set my affairs in order
I have to get out of here.
This has to end.

Hello, I'm struggling
All alone
Hello
I'm alone
Hello
I'm struggling
Hell.

SAD JANET

Everyone knows a woman
like sad Janet Jardine.
She was once young,
she was once feisty,
she was once certain.

Life has treated her harshly,
even though she choose loyalty
over self-centred want.
She stuck fast
to her commitments.

On that path
she lost her sense of purpose,
she gave up her dreams,
she sacrificed her future,
Her life given to others.

Poor Janet Jardine is sad.
She is not bitter,
she is not angry,
she is not a victim,
yet Janet Jardine sighs.

Everyone pities a woman
like sad Janet Jardine
when they hear her sigh
for the path not taken
and a life not lived.

ESCAPE

She was packing to run away.
She needed her freedom
for the good of her mind and soul.

She was going some place else,
she knew it was a crazy idea
but she didn't care.

She wanted to escape
from the mundane reality
of her current existence.

She was through with
the pressures and expectations
that weighed her down.

She had reached the end
of the road, so was
taking a leap into the unknown.

She wanted to feel the tempestuous
pulse of unknown challenge,
risking everything.

LUXURY

To her poverty was a relative thing,
She had become poor recently,
but it was only a lack
of material things
and she could manage that.

To her luxury was a new companion,
she had her own private space
an oasis of peace and calm
that provided escape
from snarling arguments.

SILVER SURFER

She sometimes wondered
how she had ended up
where she was.

It was ridiculous for
a middle-aged woman
to be sofa surfing.

Although, to be fair
she was currently
sleeping in a bed.

Albeit sharing a room
with her friend's daughter,
who was a teenager.

She had been married twice,
walking away both times
with just her suitcase.

She was always more
careful of her dignity
than financial stuff.

She sometimes wondered
whether freedom was worth it,
never reaching a conclusion.

LET IT GO

She carried it in her cupped hands,
it was still only a small seed
yet seeds had a habit of growing.

She took it out into the back garden
and released it into the air
with an exaggerated throwing motion.

The small seed of self doubt was captured
by the wind and carried away, flying
above the trees until it was lost to sight.

LOST BABIES

The shadows in her eyes
had set their place long ago,
Each one a baby carried
and then lost

The endless loops of their hope
played in her head.
They all had names,
yet no burial place.

The eldest was a boy,
He played football
a butcher, a baker or banker,
It wouldn't have mattered.

A little girl came later
Went to ballet classes
a doctor, teacher or model
She had choices.

The next baby was a boy
He liked climbing
A solider, sailor or explorer
He was adventurous.

So it went on each day.
Those potential people
Remembered,
always more than
lost babies.

NEW DAY

It was dawn with
the sky was the colour
of red sunset
yet giving no warmth.

She shivered as she watched
a new day beginning
on the eastern horizon
through the window.

The past was over
she had closed it off,
like letting the heavy cover
of an old book fall.

Yet there were times
when it seeped out,
brushing up against
the here and now.

She took the seeking tendrils
of her old life
and pushed them back
to a nowhere place.

She hadn't forgotten,
although she had tried.
Now she just didn't want to
remember the whole of it.

SANCTUARY

She told people they wouldn't believe
the story of her first marriage
and the links to the place
she now called home.

When she was a child
the house belonged to the parents
of her best friend at school.
Then they grew up, but not apart.

She got married to a pharmacist,
a good looking guy
with oodles of charm
and the gift of the gab.

They lived in a flat
above the little chemist shop
in the High Street
of a sleepy, country town.

The trouble started after
the baby was born.
The violence chilling
due to its casual delivery.

She fled the day he dangled
their baby daughter by her legs
and offered to dash her brains out
against the kitchen wall.

She ended up on the doorstep
of her best friend's mum,
incoherent with shock and fear,
seeking safety for mother and child.

She stayed for years,
unintentionally,
until she met someone else
and moved in with him.

Time passed and so did the mum,
her best friend
offered the place to them.
They eagerly brought it.

She told people they wouldn't believe
the story of why
she and her husband named
their home "Sanctuary".

A SPECIAL PLACE

Her special place changed with the light
as it moved around the room.
In the morning, she would sit
at an old fashioned desk
on a very modern swivel chair,
tapping away at her worn-out keyboard.

On the shelf above the books
is collection of Buddha statuettes
in jade, wood and ivory
and a figurine of my Lord Ganesha.
Stretching her neck to look up
she can see the Arts and Craft ceiling.

Turning to look out of the bay window,
is a view of the green lawn,
leading the eye to the wooden bridge
that crosses over the fish pond
and the stand of ancient oaks,
one branch hosting an old rope swing.

Later in the day, she rested on the fireside sofa,
angled towards the wood burning stove
whether it was alight or not,
with her books, pens and tea
on the ghost coffee table,
packed beneath with board games.

She knows
her special place
is this room,
in this house
in this tranquillity.
Just being.

INSIDE OUT

When she turn herself inside out,
to examine the hidden depths of her being,
She saw the blurred shadows
of things that she had nearly forgotten,
but their imprint remained
as a record, nevertheless.

Being inside out was not as awful
as it might sound.
There was no obvious
blood, muscle or bone.
Instead, what was displayed
was her vulnerable soul.

She was surprisingly fairer,
yet darker, than when she was
the other way around.
An elfin figure of light and shade:
Now you see her
Now you don't!

There was also, perhaps,
a hint of furled wings,
a reminder of the realms
left behind to become flesh,
ready to be spread wide
again, one day.

KINTSUGI

On the outside she looked
fine,
whole and unblemished,
But on the inside
she was a map of tiny cracks.
She liked to think
her hidden wounds
were filled with gold
Kintsugi
making her a work of art.

LADY IN GREEN

She was dressed in a leaf green cloak,
reminding me of fairy stories.
It was made of corduroy fabric
inviting hands to stroke it.

The hood was thrown back
to reveal her thick grey hair.
A circlet of silver stars
showing against her forehead.

She sat very still in the old chapel,
her eyes focused on something
not visible to other's gaze,
beyond the ancient stones.

Hers lips moved rhythmically,
as if reciting a well remembered chant,
her incantation was measured,
not hurried, nor passionate.

During all the time that I was there,
sweeping the floor and
tidying away the spent candles,
she didn't seem to notice me.

It was only back home, later,
that I wished I had spoken,
although whilst I was there
it was as if I was enchanted.

YONDER VOICE

She was listening
to the breeze
sighing through trees.

She was listening
to the sound beyond
the softly falling rain.

She could hear whispers
telling her something
she needed to know.

LADY ISABELLA

She reminded me of the little boat
that we played on
during the long, hot summers.
The whole gang of us
making our way to the creek
to sit aboard the Lady Isabella.

She rested on sticky, grey mud
when the tide was low
or bobbed up and down upon the waves
as the briny waters pushed her up.
This one had the same slim, elegant lines
as our wooden boat.

In that moment, I could smell
the ozone of the salty sea air,
I caught the sound of our laughter,
echoing down the years.
I remembered us as the bright children
we were back then.

They whispered their names
and I saw each of them,
dressed in our summer uniform
of shorts, tee shirts and sandals.
Then I was saddened that I didn't know
where any of them were now.

BACK THEN

Back then, there had been few people
on our street with a telephone in the house.
It had to be a dire emergency
for a neighbour to ask to use it.

The red telephone box was opposite
the row of shops, along the main road:
The hairdressers, fish and chip shop
green grocer, general store, drapers,
Sweet shop and the off licence.

Anyone using the telephone box
would hold open the door with one foot
to allow fresh air to circulate,
as the inside always smelt of urine.

Achieving the ventilation trick
required contortions of the body,
Since the apparatus was sited
an awkward distance from the door.

Sometimes, a few panes of glass
were smashed, but whether
due to vandalism or suffocation
it was hard to tell.

Back then, there were few people
to call, because telephones
were exceptional household items,
but red telephone boxes were common.

THE ORIENT EXPRESS

The Orient Express was a train journey
from a different era
to places that were exotically alien
and glamorous.

Smart compartments with banquettes
in rich, dark velvet,
flicking lamps with fringed shades
and crisp, white cotton head rests.

The rocking, soothing ride
began in the city of Paris.
A transcontinental odyssey
offering speed and luxury.

After leaving the canals
of watery Venice behind,
the final destination was
cosmopolitan Istanbul.

LEAVE THE PAST

There are some people
in this world
that define themselves
by something in their past.

They should, perhaps,
have more of a care -
their self limiting description
chains them to that place.

Everyone is the sum total
of their life lived to the present.
Everyone will have tales of
love gained and lost.

There will be a few regrets
happy, sparkling memories,
searing, dark spots kept hidden,
all part of life being lived.

A contented person
seems to be the one
that accepts their lot
and still moves forward.

STEPPING STONES

The Shaman spoke:
"In your mind
take the next move
onto a stepping stone.
A place to see things
from a different angle".

The Shaman spoke:
"With your body
take a while to breathe
to rest and think.
Relax in a
sanctuary of calm".

The Shaman spoke:
"Let your spirit
communicate,
through instinct
and intuition,
at one with the universe".

ANGELS SING

On those days that I have
thoughts that take me higher,
I tread softly on clouds,
I weave and wander
until I reach the gateway
to where the angels sing.

I rest comfortably
in the soft golden glow
of diffused sunlight,
I listen to the host
as they create
a new melody.

RAINBOW DAYS

The best days have rainbows,
big, bright, sturdy rainbows
that you can reach -
not for the pot of gold
kept at the end

But for the pleasure
of wishing yourself
at the top and then,
sliding down to the ground
through glistening colours

Caressing jewel-bright droplets
as you glide past on the
soft cushion of a cloud
to reach a summer day
and a sunlit shore.

FLYING

A little boy felt his heart
beating wildly in his chest
as he ran up the shallow
stone steps,
leading from the beach
to the promenade above.

He had dreamed of flying
of feeling the wind
lift him towards the sky
like a bird,
catching the air currents
and gliding on the breeze.

"Look at me" he called
to his dad below
as he leapt off,
His thin arms spread wide.
His dad caught him
before he reached the sand.

THE GATE

The boys had ridden their bikes
down the track to the beach
and back, most days,
during the summer holidays.
They hadn't noticed the gate before.
It stood, supported by
strong wooden posts
on the edge of a field
that lay empty, fallow.

Oddly, there was no fence
either side of the gate,
it was just there,
A gate into a broad meadow.
They stopped to look at it,
they teased each other
about going through it
to see what was behind it,
even though they could see.

They spread out into a line,
one brave lad directly in front
of the closed gate
and a couple either side
of the wooden posts.
The youngest boy stayed behind
to guards the bikes
The brave lad lifted the latch
and went through the gate.

FEEL THE FEAR

They called him an adrenaline junkie,
but it was when he knew he was alive.
Those times he challenged himself
to do something exciting
and experience the tempestuous
beat of his impassioned heart.

It wasn't the same feverish pulse
when he was angry or in love,
or taking recreational drugs.
It only happened when he felt
both excited and scared, all at once.

He lived for the sensation
of his heart beating faster
and stronger than usual,
feeling his body alert.
It just made him feel good.

EMPTINESS

He opened his eyes
So he could see
Something
Anything
In the blackness.

It was quiet
It was dark
And too empty
He was getting scared
It was eerie.

Something touched his arm
His mind jumped
His pulse raced
His heart thumped
Then he screamed.

DARE

She closed her eyes
so she couldn't see.
The wind blew thro' her hair,
pushing against her back.
her toes curled around
the edge of the cliff.
This was her challenge
to herself.
If she faltered
she would plunge down
to the rocky shore below.

PERSONAL TRAINER

She loved the feeling
of her racing pulse
when she was in the gym.
It was something exciting,
it made her feel alive,
unstoppable and full of energy.

Whether it was building or toning
she always weight trained
to get her heart pumping,
to get the thrill of adrenaline
coursing in her veins,
that vital throb a sign of her passion.

ONLY CLOUDS

A guy was driving along a country road.
It was a public holiday
so the roads were pretty clear.

He wasn't sure at what point
he noticed the cloud,
shaped like a flying saucer.

It looked just like one
from a comic or sci-fi mag
with exhaust fumes on the left.

He tried to keep track of it
whilst still driving,
it seemed to be keeping pace.

Then he saw several more clouds,
shaped like flying sauces
and another couple, higher up.

He woke up in hospital,
having rolled his car into a ditch
on an unnoticed, sharp bend.

CONTAMINATED SPACE

The overhead light
threw its artificial glare
over the room,
yet the space
was not sterile.

The patient lay still
except for the jerking
movement of eyes,
he was seeing
what was really there.

INTERNAL TUNE

The tune played
a continuous loop
inside his head.
Round and round
on and on
Boom, thud, boom.

He tried singing it
out loud
to exorcise it.
Boom, thud, boom,
but the tune stayed
when he stopped.

It followed him to bed
Boom, thud, boom,
keeping him awake
as he matched
his breathing
to the rhythm.

Half asleep and
ready to scream
he realised that
he was listening
to his own heartbeat
Boom, thud, boom.

MISTAKE

It only takes one mistake
to cause trouble.
Her first mistake was to stay
out with her mates,
touring the bars of London.

She got on the underground,
slightly tipsy, and that
was a mistake too
as she didn't pay enough
attention to her surroundings
and she might have dozed off.

She choose the middle carriage
of the train home,
which was another mistake
as a bloke got in a bit later
and threw up over his own shoes.

She got out at the right station
and saw the bus home waiting.
She searched her handbag
for her purse or any cash
but her money was gone.

The bus driver was not sympathetic,
he wouldn't let her get on the bus.
Her mum said it was bad to curse,
but she hoped
he would lose a few nights sleep.

She started the long walk home,
clutching her door keys in her hand
all the way, jumping at shadows.
She kept to the main roads,
despite it being a longer walk.

She got to the door of the lobby
of her block of flats,
some idiot had left it on the latch.
She got inside and locked it
then the lights went out.

HER FACE

Her face just missed being beautiful
her eyes were wide spaced,
her mouth was soft and generous.
Perhaps, it was her nose,
which was too narrow
making her merely ordinary.

It was only after an accident
that she became alluring.
A deep scar ploughed a trench
across her cheek,
it wasn't puckered
nor was it red and angry.

She worn her blemish like a trophy,
a challenge to onlookers.
She was confident in being different,
she glowed with inner certainty.
A face transformed from ordinary
to striking.

PARTY TIME

She was just tidying up her hair
in the mirror of the dressing table
when one of the party guests
wandered into the bedroom.
It was a friend of a friend
part of the crowd from the pub.

He sat on the old fashioned bed
and patted the space next to him
"Talk to me" he said.
"The previous owner of this flat
died in that bed" she told him.
He leapt up and ran away.

THE RIGHT JOB

Rachel had taken a job
as a waitress in the bistro
as a way of meeting new people.
It wasn't a transport cafe
like her granddad loved.
It wasn't a pub
like her brother loved.
It was smart lunches by day
and smarter dinners by night.

So far, it hadn't work out
as she thought it would,
People didn't notice the waitress,
people didn't talk with her,
except to place orders
or ask where the toilet was.
There were no longer transport cafes,
but there were pubs where
customers talked to the staff.

MEET ME

Amy's phone pinged with a message
number not recognised:
"Meet me at the cemetery gates
this afternoon at two, beautiful Amy".

She was intrigued,
no one had called her beautiful
since her skiing accident
when her leg had shattered.

She wondered who it could be,
she didn't meet many people,
she didn't go out much,
her walking stick made it awkward.

She would go, she decided,
she could watch from the bus shelter
to see who turned up.
It was a good place for sitting.

At the appointed time,
she saw her sister's boyfriend,
hanging about the cemetery gates.
She liked him, but....

ANNIE'S BAR

The formal name of the place is
Artazier Beauty Rooms,
but in local legend
it's called Annie's Bar.

It's in an out of the way
and hidden courtyard
just off the High Street
down a wide alley.

The interior is deep purple
with glinting copper highlights
and bottles and bottles of
nail colours in picture frames.

The chatelaine is magnificent Annie
of the long, dark and tumbling hair,
a cheerful, bubbly woman
who fills the space with energy.

Annie is renowned for her
early morning broadcasts,
where she shares beauty routines
or her dog walks in the park.

She loves designing
tiny fruits, flowers or patterns
on carefully prepared nails
painted in fashionable hues.

Annie showcases her creations
on social media and her website,
attracting new customers
wanting her miniature artwork.

When you step into the
Artazier Beauty Rooms
you become part of the
legend that is Annie's Bar.

FARMER

He walked past the pavement cafe,
A man of the land
with a weather-beaten face
of polished wood,
etched with creases from
the sun and wind,
his eyes bright and shiny.

His rolling gait whispered of
hours spent in the saddle.
A man from any time or place,
dressed in blue jeans, brown boots
and an ironed work shirt
with sleeves rolled up
to above his elbows.

Despite his advanced age,
he looked sprightly enough
to manage a day labouring
on the land or herding beasts.
A man at ease with life
striding through the town
on a private quest.

TOXIC AIR

The ladies at the Women's Institute meeting
were milling around during the tea break.
One of the Committee members called out
"I can smell Jo Malone,
whose wearing perfume?"
No one gave an immediate response.
A new lady approached the
Committee member and told her,
shyly, that she was wearing
Neroli with sweet almond oil
a blend that she mixed herself.
The Committee member responded
dismissively, "It can't be that"
and turned away.

INSECT BITES

"I've got another mosquito bite" she wailed
"Where this time?" he asked
"Just above my knee" she told him
"How's the one on your face?" he asked
"Okay, almost gone" she replied
"And the one on your foot?" he enquired
"Much better, thanks.
It still itches sometimes" she said
"I think it was an ant" he mused
"Great, blood sucking ants now" she cried
"No. It would have been
A sting" he said

"How come all these critters
head for me and not you?" she asked
"Thick skin and Marmite.
You should have Marmite
on toast for breakfast
like I do" he suggested
"No, I have bread for lunch.
Too much stodgy food
isn't healthy" she replied
"I'm not so sure about that.
I haven't been bitten" he said.

MINT

The whole kitchen was filled
with the aroma of herbage.
"What's happening here?" he asked
"I cut back the mint, so it wouldn't go to seed.
Doesn't it smell fresh?"
"It smells" he said "like toothpaste".

"What are you going to do with it all?
he asked
"Wash it, dry it and chop it.
Then put in in the freezer"
So we don't have any fresh mint left?"
he asked.

"Yes, of course we do, silly.
This is just extra"
"Hmm, so when are we going
to use the extra, frozen mint
when we always have fresh mint?"
he asked.

POTATO SALAD

"There's not quite enough mayonnaise
for the potato salad, so I'm going
to add a spoonful of tartare sauce" he said
"Okay" she replied.

"We don't have any chives,
so I'm going to add some
thinly chopped, red onion" he said
"Okay" she replied.

"We've run out of wombat
so I'm going to add echidna
instead" he said
"Okay" she replied.

MOWING THE LAWN

"I nearly cut all the grass" he said
"I just didn't do a strip at the front"

She looked out at the front lawn
"I can't see any long bits" she said

"Not that front" he said
"It's the only front we have" she replied

"I meant the front out the back" he said
"We don't have a front out back" she said

"I know where I've mowed" he said
She shrugged

She was never going to understand
his method of cataloguing the garden.

CLEANING WITH COLA

"I've got timescale in the toilet.
I've tried everything to shift it" moaned Jo
"What's everything?" asked Ros
"You know, whatever they sell
in the supermarket" replied Jo
"You've been looking in the wrong aisle.
You need a can of cola" said Ros
"What?" puzzled Jo
"It's easy enough.
You scoop out as much water
from the bowl as possible.
Then pour in the cola
and leave it overnight."
"I've never heard that one" said Jo
"It's a really effective cleaner.
If you don't believe me,
Put a dirty, old 2p coin in a saucer
and cover it with cola.
Leave it for a couple of minutes.
See what happens."
"If it cleans old coins, I wonder
what it does to your insides" said Jo.

CIDER DRINKERS

"Do you remember all the cider
we drank when we were younger" asked Ros
"Oh yes! It's only recently
that I can bear the smell" replied Jo
"So is there anything worse
for getting drunk on?" wondered Ros
"I can't face Pernod. I was so sick, all night.
What about you?" said Jo
"Dark rum. There was an old bottle
at the back of the cupboard
in my mum and dad's kitchen
that I drank with Simon Peters.
You know the guy I went out with for a while."
said Ros
"Wow! I'd forgotten about you and Simon Peters.
What did happen there?" asked Jo
"Maybe I'll tell you one day" teased Ros.

FRIENDS

Three old chaps met up
at the pub occasionally.
It was something they'd done
over the years,
since leaving school.

One had scooted off
to the gents.
His mate turned to
the other one
and sniffed.

"Old Don" he said
"Chucks up a bit nowadays.
I reckon we might forget
to let him know next time"
His friend winked.

AN OUTING

A coach company ran regular
coach trips between Easter and September.
They had a strong core of loyal explorers
that travelled every month.

Hannah rather enjoyed driving them,
as they were jolly and tipped well.
Generally, they were no trouble
and were respectful of the rules.

Yet, today she felt she'd picked up
the wrong passengers
or they'd got on the wrong bus.
They all seemed to be suffering.

The first guy on was wearing shorts,
so everyone could see his ulcer
without the bother of him
rolling up his trouser leg.

A bit later an obese woman
had to be heaved and shoved
up the three short steps,
leaving everyone tired and sweaty.

The same procedure had to be repeated
for a lady with an arthritic knee.
She was on the waiting list
for a replacement and a hernia op.

Next came two women,
who looked red-eyed
due to being hungover, they claimed
and not an emotional drama.

Another woman was worried
about her hearing aids,
as she could hear whooshing,
so she took them out.

The old major-type was walking stiffly.
He'd tripped and caught his lower back
on the tow bar of his Volvo
which had set off his piles.

Hannah wondered whether
she would be sacked if she took them
to hospital, rather than Margate,
otherwise, it would be a long day.

BRIEF ENCOUNTER

A woman had just left a cafe.
She was walking up the street
back towards her car.
"Excuse me" a voice said behind her
"I just wanted to say, I love your handbag"
"Oh" said the woman
"Thank you." Being polite.

"How do I look?" asked the stranger
"Like someone with bright, pink hair"
said the woman, thinking
This is bizarre.
"Only I'm meeting someone and
It's our first date. He's a policeman"
continued the stranger.

"I hope it goes well" said the woman
"He knows I'm trans" said the stranger
"I stopped to have coffee, because
I'm nervous. Do you think he'll like me?"
"He wouldn't be meeting you,
If he didn't like you" said the woman
as she started to walk again.

"We set it up on the internet"
confided the stranger,
as they both walked along
"That's not unusual nowadays,
I think" said the woman.
"But I look alright? insisted the stranger
"Yes, fine" said the woman.

"I'm not a fan of pink hair" she added
"But if you like it, that's okay"
"I'm usually blonde, but
I wanted a change" said the stranger
"It happens to us all, sometimes "
responded the woman, adding
"I need to cross the road here".

"It's been nice talking to you"
said the stranger
"And to you" said the woman
"I really hope you have a nice date"
"So do I" replied the stranger
"Cheerio, then"
"Bye" said the woman.

BIKERS

The bikers were gathering
at the Conservative Club.
It seemed incongruous -
a chapter of possible
'Hell's Angels'
in an establishment car park.

They were dressed in
black leather and blue denim,
their helmets had full visors
hiding faces,
their machines were
big and loud.

They began to take off headgear
and remove their leathers,
making them less menacing and
revealing hair in many shades of grey
and bodies past their prime.

Then is seemed reasonable,
perhaps even inevitable,
for bikers of middle years
and beyond
to be in the car park
of the Conservative Club.

SEAFARERS

They are the riders of the waves
The surfers of the tides,
They are the men who
go down to the sea in ships.

They travel the ocean deep,
following old trade routes
long ago discovered
by their ancestors.

They are the heroes of sea battles
against villains, monsters and ice.
They discover new wonders
Adventurers, brave and strong.

CAT PRESENT

The clock read 2.22
so it was the middle of the night.
The cat wasn't in his usual place,
but there was an indent
in the bed covers where
he had slept earlier.

His owner searched every room,
which didn't take long
as it was a small place,
but the cat wasn't at home.
The owner flipped the cat flap
to make sure it was working.

Later, the cat was back,
thumping himself heavily
down on the bed,
knowing it would cause
the human to wake up
and give some attention.

The cat arched its back
in a long, elegant stretch,
waiting for the human
to notice the headless mouse
that he had carefully
laid on the bed covers.

PIGS

The pig arcs were scattered
across the muddy field,
looking like fungi
sprung from the earth.

The wood had a pinkish hue,
as if it had absorbed
the flesh colour
of the snuffling hogs.

A village of low arches,
providing shelter
to a whole herd
of swine and piglets.

They looked robust beasts,
nosing in the troughs,
wallowing in the mire.
Happy until market day.

LOST DOG

The dog trotted up the lane
A poodle cross of some sort
with a curly brown coat.
An owner was nowhere to be seen,
the animal had slipped out,
unnoticed from his home.

The car stopped a little distance
from the adventurous dog.
A woman got out
and crouched down.
making soft calling noises and
holding out an aromatic treat.

The dog approached,
taking the chew from her hand.
She slipped the fingers
of her other hand
under the dog's collar
and ushered him into the car.

The door closed quietly,
then the car turned around
and drove away.
Later two children
ran the length of the lane
calling their pet's name.

SMELLY DOG

Our dog rolled in pheasant droppings again,
squirming on her back with her paws in the air,
looking totally undignified,
wallowing in abandon
in her own private world of ecstasy.

Our dog prefers fox droppings,
but they are not so readily available,
which is a good thing for us.
The smell is vile and the consistency sticky
and much tougher to wash off.

MIRROR

Looking
into a pool of clear water
there is much to see:
The whole world is mirrored there
an echo of the sunlit sky
with its passing clouds,
an image of the bountiful land
with its diverse fauna and flora.

Looking
beyond the pool of clear water
to see the fires of creation:
The molten elements of life
within the bubbling cauldron,
the spark that made an explosion
of galaxies, worlds, stars
and infinite possibility.

CREATION

Here is the morning sun,
riding up into the sky
towards its noon-time zenith.

Here is the refreshing rain,
splashing onto the earth,
quenching thirst.

Here is the gentle breeze,
tugging seeds
into the fragrant air.

Here is the world,
ripening with procreation
in flora and fauna.

Here is the cycle of life,
burgeoning into glory
before turning again.

UNICORN

The horse looked silver
in the moonlight,
as it stood next to a tree.
There was a stout twig
outlined against its forehead,
as if it were a horn,
creating the illusion
of a unicorn.

SUMMER GARDEN

The air hung heavy

With scented honeysuckle

And rich fragrant roses.

SUNFLOWERS

Sunflowers
reaching for the sky.
Brown, brown hearts
deep and dusky centres,
framed by golden petals
overlapping,
gently shaped to
sharp points,
thick green stems
stretching tall.

SUMMER RAIN

The thunder sounded
like a suitcase,
being wheeled over cobbles.
The rain, when it came,
was of big drops falling softly.
There was no lightning.
Then it was over,
leaving no impression
at all.

BECALMED

It was one of those days
when the air is hot and heavy,
when sweat sticks to the skin
in damp, prickly patches.

The thunder boomed across the sky,
the wind picked up,
snatching petals from blossom,
creating an expectation of rain.

Then it was silent,
not a hint of thunder,
not the slightest breeze,
the oppressive heat returned.

AFTER THE STORM

The wind was blowing
across the bare fields,
buffeting the remaining clouds
across the sky that was
still washed out
from yesterday's storm.

The sun shone briefly
intermittent golden rays,
before being obscured
by the stubborn grey.
of another dull day,
yet the birds were singing.

HARVEST GOLD

The crops had been harvested

The dust causing a haze

Over the denuded fields.

The remaining stubble

Leaving the land

Still rich and golden.

PUGLIA, ITALY

The colours of Puglia are magical,
because they uplift the spirits.
You just feel joyful when you see
The happy orange of pomegranate,
The merry purple of lavender and
The festive scarlet of wild poppies.

The sounds of Puglia are enchanting,
because they are spellbinding.
You just feel charmed when you hear
The tuneful clang of goat bells,
The hiccuping bray of donkeys and
The musical voices of the people.

The aromas of Puglia are bewitching,
because they are medicine for the mind.
You just feel relaxed when you smell
The bouquet of gentle Italian herbs,
The fragrant smoke of olive wood fires
And the delicate scent of flowers.

The ambience of Puglia is blissful,
because it allows your soul to breath.
You just feel deep contentment there
The atmosphere makes the heart sing,
The air makes the feet dance
And peace settles all around you.

LAVENDER IN PROVENCE

Lavender in Provence blooms in the summer
fields and fields of purple flowers,
stretching for miles across the landscape.
The air is filled with its fragrance
slightly herbal, medicinal, lazy.

Lavender in Provence is beautiful
creating a dreamy atmosphere.
Yellow and black bees are busy,
humming, buzzing and dancing
between the plants against a blue sky.

ZANZIBAR

Zanzibar is a spice island
Situated in the Indian Ocean.
Its capital is Stone Town
A World Heritage Site.

Zanzibar is a spice island
But it smells of life
People, food, bitumen torches
And seaweed.

It is an exotic contrivance
Wide-eyed, skinny children
People in bright clothing,
Selling nutmeg and cinnamon.

Situated in the Indian Ocean
A sea of turquoise water,
Beaches of white sand
Off the coast of Africa.

On a coast road
Is the restaurant shack
Of Freddie Mercury's uncle,
Serving fresh sea food.

Its capital is Stone Town
Bustling, busy streets
Voices speaking Swahili,
Arabic and tourist lingoes.

Zanzibar was essential
For the slave trade,
Taking captives from Africa
To the Middle East.

A World Heritage Site
With old Arab trader buildings,
Colonial houses and churches
And the Night Market.

There is a wonderful museum
Full of household items,
Formica and G-Plan furniture
And classic cars.

Zanzibar is spice
Turquoise ocean
Historic cultures
Exotic dreaming.

LIGHT

I like the light
bright or subdued
Moonlight
and sunlight

I don't mind the dark
inky or dappled
Lapping around the edges
of a silent world

I like the light more
than the dark
The clarity of distant horizon
The glory of bright colour.

BIRD WATCHING

The garden was alive with birds
that late spring morning.
Parson Pie had swooped down
with his partner, Maggie,
looking stylish in black and white.

Mrs Hubbard and her crew
of Timmy, Tommy and Trudy
with Bobby, Bernie and Ben
had exercised on the grass
their pigeon feathers iridescent.

Sir Robin had perched himself
on the wooden bench by a tree,
watching with lazy curiosity.
Lady Redbreast was nowhere
to be seen so early in the day.

Baron Black pecked in the lawn
sis feathers as dark as any crow
as he stopped to feast on worm.
His wife hopped out from the hedge
dressed in her brown drab.

The garden was alive with birds
that late spring morning
The birds may not have been rare
but their lives were stories
made for entertaining.

YELLOW BIRD

A woman was in the village shop,
She told the post mistress
that if anyone had lost a canary
it was in the woods.

The man who organised walks
overheard the conversation.
He said that the bird
was likely to be a yellowhammer.

They usually nested just outside
the village boundary on farmland.
They all agreed a wild bird was
far more exciting than a canary.

RIVER BIRDS

The walk along the riverbank
on a slow and lazy morning
had a soft, magical air.
It was early enough for a mist
to still be rising from the water.

The kingfisher appeared
from a clump of bushes
and performed a ballet dance
of rising, diving and turning
in the delicate moisture.

Later, a swan had come into view
gliding along in effortless majesty.
A mystical creature escaped
from a half remembered fairy tale
so impossibly elegant.

Nearing the village.
a whole host of mallard ducks
were gathering on the water
to enjoy a feast together
on a slow, lazy morning.

TRUE COLOURS

His body was copper,
speckled with cream feathers,
a forest green head
merging into blue
at his slender neck.

He wore an eye mask
of poppy red felt
that he peered out from
with coal black, shiny eyes.

His long tail feathers
were all shades of coffee.
A colourful creature
of the countryside.
A bird called pheasant.

BREAKFAST

She noticed him under the tree
a darker shape
against the oak's shade.
He had moved closer to the lawn
by the time she had returned
to the paved terrace
with a beaker of bird food.

He watched with his head held high
as she shook out the contents
across the grass.
She retreated into the house,
looking through a window,
as he ran straight-legged
and comical to his breakfast.

He had a routine of watchfulness
Peck, peck, look right
Peck, peck, peck, head up
Vigilant, alert to potential danger
Peck, peck, look left.
When his appetite was sated
he stalked back to the tree
on his thin, stiff legs
merging with the shadows.

GARISH YELLOW

The birds were thrilling a cheerful chorus
The clouds were dripping silver rain
The countryside was looking glorious
The hedgerows were a rich, velvet green
The fields were of mellow gold cereal
Suddenly
The garish yellow of rape seed flowers
Struck a jarring note
Amid the gentle hues of the landscape.

LEMONS

Lemons grow on trees,
it is perfectly true
but what is less well known
is that citrus trees are difficult
to establish.

Lemons will only grow
in a place that is sunny,
but also sheltered from the wind.
The trees need to be happy
to produce fruit.

A contented lemon tree
will produce white flowers
with a hint of yellow edging.
The blooms are beautiful, although
not as fragrant as orange blossom.

At first, the fruit resembles a rose-hip
swelling and growing day-by-day
in the summer heat,
until it turns bright yellow
and is ready to fall.

TREE OF LOVE

Love is living and growing

It is the fruit of life

And, like a well-tended tree,

It gives more when it is

Encouraged to grow.

AUTUMN LEAVES

The leaves beneath my feet
are dry and crisp
They crunch as I walk over them.

These leaves are of the autumn
In rich hues of red, brown and orange
blown from stately trees.

The leaves are a reminder
that another season is passing,
making way for chilling winter.

SOUP

The weather was cooler now,
So it was time for home-made soup.
The butternut squash
Was a soft peach colour
That went well with vermilion
Of the sweet potatoes
And deep red of the onions.

The chopped onion and garlic
Released a tantalising aroma,
As they softened slowly
In the big pan, over a low heat.
The squash and sweet potatoes
Had been peeled and chopped
And went into the pan too.

The last ingredient was a jug
Of vegetable stock made from cubes
That was stirred into the pan
And gently brought to a simmer.
It would take a couple of hours
Before the soup could be mashed
To a smooth consistency.

Yet, it would be ready for lunch
To be served with crusty bread
That had been baked during the night
By the machine in the kitchen.
Orange soup topped with black pepper
Would taste delicious
With the golden loaf.

MOVING ON

These days, she trod
so lightly on the earth
that her footsteps
left no mark.

She moved
so softly through crowds
that none remarked
her presence.

She watched the world
so quietly
that none noticed
Her gaze.

Yet, it wasn't
always this way,
she had somehow
grown apart.

With the passing
of her years
She had left behind
possession and desire.

This shedding of want
had laid bare
the essence of
an old soul.

She was gently
moving back
to become part of
the greater universe.

MY MOTHER IS IN THE EARTH

My mother is in the earth,
she was an occasional Catholic
particularly when it suited her.
With regard to her mortal remains
she choose to invoke
her religious leaning.

My mother had a green burial
she lies in a wicker casket
dressed in her linen shroud
under newly planted trees
laced with English bluebells
without a grave marker.

IS ANYONE THERE?

It was like looking at the world
through water,
it was definitely there
she could almost see it,
But as she tried to
make out the detail
it broke up into a kaleidoscope
of muted colours.
She called out
"Can you see me?"
But there was no response.

She tried to concentrate
on the sounds,
though they were faint,
some noises were distorted
with an erratic hum
in the background.
Her voice sounded papery
even to her own ears.
She called out
"Can you hear me?"
But there was no response.

It was like being separated
from the world
by very thick glass.
No one seemed to see her
when she stood close.
No one seemed to hear her
when she spoke
right next to their ear.
But then
She was still
A very new ghost.

VIBRATION

Everything vibrates
It is cosmic energy

Mortals vibrate
Nature vibrates

The universe vibrates
So vibration is being.

Printed in Great Britain
by Amazon